THE MYSTERIES OF FASTING

Other books translated by the author:

(1) The Book of Knowledge
(2) The Foundations of the Articles of Faith
(3) The Mysteries of Purity

Our other publications about Ghazzali:

1. Al-Ghazzali on Divine Predicates and their Properties
2. Some Moral and Religious Teachings of Ghazzali
3. Faith and Practice of Ghazzali
4. The Ethical Philosophy of Al-Ghazzali
5. The Confessions of Al-Ghazzali
6. Ghazzali's Mishkat al-Anwar
7. The Alchemy of Happiness

THE MYSTERIES OF FASTING

BEING A TRANSLATION WITH NOTES

of

The Kitāb Asrār al-Ṣawm

of

Al-Ghazzāli's "Iḥyā' 'Ulūm al-Dīn"

By
NABIH AMIN FARIS
AMERICAN UNIVERSITY OF BEIRUT

SH. MUHAMMAD ASHRAF
PUBLISHERS, BOOKSELLERS & EXPORTERS
7-Aibak Road (New Anarkali) LAHORE-7 (Pak)

Reprinted..................1987.

Printed & Bound at
NEW WORLD PRINTERS
7-Aibak Road (New Anarkali)
LAHORE-7 (Pak)

Published by :
SH. SHAHZAD RIAZ
For SH. MUHAMMAD ASHRAF
Publishers & Booksellers,
7-Aibak Road (New Anarkali)
Lahore-7 (Pak)

PREFACE

The practice of fasting as a spiritual discipline is both ancient and widespread. It antedates Islam, even among the Arabs, and from time immemorial has been observed in various ways by Jews, Christians, and eastern and pagan religions. The Prophet himself, according to several authentic traditions[1] was wont to observe, like his own tribe of Quraysh, the fast of 'Āshūrā' on the tenth day of Muḥarram. The custom was taken over from the Jewish 'āsōr fast of the Day of Atonement, which fell on the tenth of Tishrī. "When the Prophet came to Medina he found the Jews fasting on the Day of 'Āshūrā'. When they were asked about it they said: 'This is the Day on which God gave victory to Moses and the children of Israel over Pharaoh, so we keep it as a fast to honour it'. The Prophet replied: 'We are more worthy of Moses than you are', and commanded that it be kept a fast."[2] After the break

1. See Muslim, *Ṣaḥīḥ*, Dār al-Ṭibā'ah al-'Āmmah, Cairo 1330, Vol. III, pp. 146-50 ; al-Bukhāri, *Ṣaḥīḥ*, Ṣawm : 1, 69.

2. Muslim, *Ṣaḥīḥ*, Vol. III, p. 149.

with the Jews the fast of Ramaḍān was instituted, but the custom of fasting 'Āshūrā' became optional and supererogatory. It commemorates the day on which Noah left the ark.[1]

Though not one of the four pre-Islamic sacred months, namely dhu-'l-Qa'dah, dhu-'l-Ḥijjah, Muḥarram, and Rajab, during which fighting was unlawful, Ramaḍān was of special religious significance among the Quraysh. Those of them who desired to do penance were accustomed to go to Mt. Ḥirā' upon the beginning of Ramaḍān where they performed their *taḥannuth* (religious devotion and penance). The exercises lasted the entire month, and at its conclusion the devotees made their way to the Kaaba where they performed the circumambulation seven times and then returned home to resume normal life. The Prophet himself observed the same custom.[2] And it was during one of those vigils of devotion and penance in Ramaḍān that the Prophet received his first divine revelation.[3] The Qur'ān specifically states

1. Ibn-al-Athīr, *al-Kāmil fi-'l-Tārīkh*, Cairo 1303, Vol. I, p. 25.

2. Ibn-Hishām, *Sīrat Rasūl Allāh*, ed. F. Wustenfeld, Leyden, 1858-1860, pp. 151-52; tr. A. Guillaume, Oxford University Press, 1955, pp 105-6; al-Balādhurī, *Ansāb al-Ashrāf*, ed. M. Ḥamīd Allāh, Cairo 1959, p. 105.

3. Ibn-Hishām, p. 152.

this, and links the institution of Ramaḍān as the proper month of fasting for Muslims with the month "wherein the Qur'ān was sent down to be a guidance to the people, and as a clear sign of Guidance and Salvation."[1] The night on which the first revelation took place is known as the Laylat al-Qadr (the Night of Power), "which is better than a thousand months; in it the angels and the Spirit descend, by the leave of their Lord, upon every command. Peace it is, till the rising of dawn."[2] It was also in Ramaḍān that the Prophet won his first major decisive victory at Badr, which was interpreted as the divine sanction of the new faith,[3] the miraculous Furqān[4] which distinguished good from evil. For all these reasons, the institution of Ramaḍān as the proper month of fasting became quite natural. The battle of Badr took place in Ramaḍān, A H. 2 [February-March A.D. 624], and, in all likelihood, the fast of Ramaḍān to be fully observed was

1. *Sūrah* ii : 185. Quranic quotations in the *Preface* are after the translation of A. J. Arberry, Oxford 1964. Numbering of verses follow that of the Cairo edition of King Fuad, A.H. 1342.

2. *Sūrah* xcvii : 3-5.

3. *Sūrah* iii : 123.

4. *Sūrah* viii : 41 42.

that of A.H. 3 [February 15-March 16, A.D. 625].

The following pages are a translation of the *Kitāb Asrār al-Ṣawm* (On the Mysteries of Fasting) which is the fifth book of the first quarter of the *Iḥyā' 'Ulūm al-Dīn.* The translation is based on three printed texts and one in manuscript form. The printed texts are : first that printed at Kafr al-Zaghāri in A.H. 1352 from the older Cairo edition of A.H. 1289; second, that contained in the text of the *Itḥāf al-Sādah al-Muttaqīn bi-Sharḥ Iḥyā' 'Ulūm al-Dīn* of al-Sayyid al-Murtaḍā al-Zabīdi (d. 1791); third, that reproduced in the margin of the same *Itḥāf al-Sādah*; and fourth, the text preserved in a four-volume manuscript in the Garrett Collection of Arabic Manuscripts in the Princeton University Library (No. 1481). In the translation of Quranic verses, I have depended mainly on J.M. Rodwell's version.

It is my hope that by making still another Book of the *Iḥyā'* available in English, non-Arabic-speaking scholars will be benefited, even from my mistakes.

Nabih Amin Faris

Beirut
February 15, 1967

BOOK VI

On the Mysteries of Fasting

INTRODUCTION

Praise be to God who hath shown great favour unto His servants by delivering them from the wiles of Satan; who hath thwarted the hopes of the devil and frustrated his designs by making fasting a bulwark and a shield for His saints; who hath opened the gates of Paradise unto them and taught them that the way of Satan to their hearts lieth in secret lust; who hath made known unto them that only through subduing its secret lust could the soul at rest assert its superiority.

In accordance with the words of the Apostle that "fasting comprises half of fortitude"[1] and "fortitude forms half of belief",[2] fasting equals one-fourth of belief. Furthermore, it is distinguished from the other pillars [of Islam] by its special and peculiar position in relation to God, since He said through the mouth of His Prophet

1. Literally *ṣabr*, i.e., patience. Unidentified.
2. Unidentified.

"Every good deed will be rewarded from ten-to-seven hundred fold except fasting which is endured for My sake and which I shall reward."[1] God also said, "Verily, the patient shall be repaid: their reward shall not be by measure."[2] Fasting comprises one-half of fortitude and its reward transcends reckoning and calculation. To have an idea of its excellence you have only to remember the words of the Apostle when he said, "By Him who holds my life in His hand, the soul breath of the fasting man's mouth is more fragrant before God and better pleasing to Him than redolent musk." 'The fasting man abjureth his food and drink and suppresseth his appetite for My sake,' said the Lord, 'and I shall reward him for it.'[3] The Apostle also said, "Verily Paradise hath, [among others], a gate which is called al-Rayyān and through which no one shall enter except those who have observed the fast."[4] And again, "Two joys are prepared for him who observes the fast; the joy of breaking the fast and that of meeting his Lord."[5] On another

1. *Cf.* al-Bukhārī, Ṣawm : 2; Muslim, Ṣiyām : 160, 162-164.
2. *Sūrah* xxxix : 13.
3. Al-Bukhārī, Ṣawm : 2, 9.
4. *Ibid.*, Ṣawm : 4.
5. Muslim, Ṣiyām : 162, 164, 165; al-Bukhārī, Ṣawm : 9.

occasion he said, "Everything hath a gateway and the gateway of worship is fasting."[1] And again he said, "The sleep of the fasting man is worship."[2]

Abu-Hurayrah related that the Apostle once said, "When the month of Ramaḍān arriveth the gates of Paradise are flung open while those of Hell are closed. At the same time all the devils are put in chains [212] and a herald crieth out, 'O thou who seekest good come hither, and thou who desireth evil desist'."[3]

Commenting on the words of God, "Eat ye and drink with healthy relish, for what ye did aforetime in the days that have gone by,"[4] Wakī'[5] said that "the days that have gone by" were the days of fasting, since during those days [men and women] have abstained from food and drink.[6]

On another occasion the Apostle himself included the renunciation of the world and fasting [in the list of things which lift man to] the rank

1. Unidentified.
2. Unidentified.
3. Ibn-Mājah, Ṣiyām : 1.
4. *Sūrah* lxix : 24.
5. Ibn-al-Jarrāḥ, A.H. 197/A.D. 812 : ibn-Sa'd, Vol. VI, p. 275.
6. *Cf.* al-Ṭabari, *Jāmi' al-Bayān*, Vol. XXIX, p. 39.

[of the angels]. Thus he said, "Verily God will make His angels vie with the ascetic young man saying, 'O young man who hast suppressed thy carnal lust for My sake and who hast consecrated the prime of thy life unto Me, thou art in My sight as one of My angels'."[1]

And again the Apostle said that God would address His angels concerning fasting and say, "O My angels! Behold My servant: he hath suppressed his carnal lust, abjured his pleasures, and given up his food and drink—he hath done all that for My sake."[2]

Concerning the words of God "No soul knoweth what joy is reserved for them in recompense of their works,"[3] it has been said that "their works" were fasting, since God said, "Verily the patient shall be repaid: their reward shall not be by measure."[4] Thus will the reward of the fasting man be generous and even profuse and it will be beyond imagination or estimate. It is very meet that it be so, because fasting belongs to God

1. *Cf.* ibn-Mājah, Masājid : 19.
2. Unidentified.
3. *Sūrah* xxxii : 17.
4. *Sūrah* xxxix : 13.

and, by virtue of this relationship, it has been rendered noble, although all the acts of worship belong to God, just as the House (*al-Bayt*)[1] has been made noble by its special relationship to God, although the whole earth is His also. Fasting belongs to God in two respects: first, because it is a form of desisting and relinquishing, in its very nature concealed from human sight, whereas all the other acts of worship are apparent and exposed to it. It stands alone as the only act of worship which is not seen by anyone except God. It is an inward act of worship performed through sheer endurance and fortitude. Second, because it is a means of vanquishing the enemy of God, Satan, who works through the appetites and carnal lusts. These appetites and lusts are strengthened by eating and drinking. For this reason the Apostle said, "Verily Satan affects the son of Adam by pervading his blood. Let him therefore make this difficult for Satan by means of hunger."[2] For the same reason he told 'Ā'ishah, "Persist in knocking the door of Paradise." When she asked, "With what shall I knock the

1. *Al-Bayt* and *al-Bayt al-'Atīq* (the old house) denote the Ka'bah.

2. *Cf.* ibn-Mājah, Ṣiyām : 65 ; abu-Dāwūd, Ṣawm : 78.

door of Paradise?" he replied. "With hunger."[1] The excellence of hunger will be discussed under the section which deals with the evils of gluttony and the remedy therefrom [in the Book on the Two Appetites] in the Quarter on the Destructive Matters of Life.[2]

Whereas fasting is primarily a method of subduing Satan, blocking his path, and placing obstacles in his way, it deserves a special place in relation to God, since subduing the enemy of God is an aid to Him, and His aid is not forthcoming unless men aid Him. Thus He said, "If ye aid God, He will help you, and will set your feet firm."[3] The servant should take the initiative and commence his efforts and God will crown him with success by guiding him into His ways. For this reason God said, "And whoso maketh efforts for Us, in Our ways will We guide them,"[4] God also said, "Verily God changeth not what a people hath until they change it for themselves."[5] Change increases temptation and strengthens the

1. Unidentified.
2. See Vol. III, Bk. iii, sect. 1.
3. *Sūrah* xlvii : 8.
4. *Sūrah* xxix : 69.
5. *Sūrah* xiii : 12.

appetites which are the grazing grounds of the devils and their pasturing land. As long as they are fertile the devil will continue to frequent them, and as long as he frequents them the majesty of God will not be revealed to the servant and [His glory] will always remain concealed from him. The Apostle said, "Had it not been for the fact that the devils hover around the hearts of the children of Adam, the latter would have readily lifted their hearts unto the Kingdom of Heaven."[1] In this respect fasting becomes the gateway to worship and a protection [against the fires of Hell].[2]

Since its excellence has become so very important, it is necessary to describe its outward and inward conditions by enumerating its principles and regulations as well as its inward rules. We shall discuss this under three sections.

1. Unidentified.
2. *Cf.* ibn-Mājah, Ṣiyām : 1 ; al-Bukhārī, Ṣawm : 2.

SECTION I

On the Outward Duties and Regulations [of Fasting] and the Duties Attending the Breaking of it

THE OUTWARD DUTIES

The outward duties relative to fasting are six: the first duty is to watch the beginning of the month of Ramaḍān [and announce it] at the observation of the new moon (*al-hilāl*). But if the clouds should make the observation of the new moon impossible then the length of Sha'bān should be extended to thirty days. By observation we mean actual sighting [of the new moon]. It is established by the word of one veracious and trustworthy witness, while that of the new moon of Shawwāl is not established except by the word of two witnesses. This is merely a [means of] precaution for [the preservation of the purity of] worship. Anyone who hears a trustworthy witness assert that he had seen the new moon and believes him, fasting thereupon becomes incumbent upon him, even though the judge (*al-qāḍi*) should fail to announce the arrival of the new month. In the matter of worship, therefore, let each person do whatever he deems best.

Whenever the new moon is seen in one town but is not seen in another, and the distance between the two is less than two days' journey, fasting becomes incumbent upon both towns alike. But if the distance were more than two days' journey, each town would have its own arrangement, and what would be incumbent upon the one would not extend to the other.

The second outward duty is intention (*niyyah*). Every night before the dawn of the following day[1] the person should specifically and deliberately entertain the intention of fasting. If he should entertain the intention to fast [213] the month of Ramaḍān but fail to renew his intention every night, his fast would not be valid. This is what we meant when we said every night. If he should entertain the intention during the daytime his fast would not be valid. This is true of the fast of the month of Ramaḍān and of the obligatory fasts (*ṣawm al-farḍ*), but the voluntary fasts (*ṣawm al-taṭawwu'*) are excepted. This is what we meant

1. Ar. *mubayyatah*.

when we said that the intention of fasting should be entertained during the night before the day of fasting.

If he should entertain the intention to fast either the month of Ramaḍān or the obligatory fasts but fail to be specific, his fast would not be valid. The obligatory fast as well as the fast of the month of Ramaḍān are ordained by God and their observance should be the result of specific intention.

If during the doubtful night (*laylat al-shakk*)[1] he should entertain the intention to fast the following day if it should belong to Ramaḍān, then his fast would not be valid, unless his intention is supported by the word of a trustworthy witness. The possibility that the trustworthy witness (*'adl*) might be mistaken or even lying should not affect the determination of the person who has planned to fast the following day. Similarly any attendant circumstances such as doubt concerning the last night of Ramaḍān would not prevent the person from entertaining the intention to fast the following day. Nor

1. The thirtieth night in Sha'bān.

would the intention to fast be affected if its entertainment depended upon mere conjecture, as in the case of a person imprisoned in a dark dungeon, who thinks that the month of Ramaḍān had arrived; whatever doubts he might have would not prevent him from entertaining the intention to fast. Again, if a person should be uncertain of the night of doubt, the verbal expression of his intention to fast [the following day] would not avail because the seat of intention is the heart, wherein it is inconceivable to entertain doubt in conjunction with certainty. Thus if in the middle of Ramaḍān one should say that he would fast the following day if that day were of Ramaḍān, no harm could be done because it is mere repetition of words, while in the seat of intention there would be no room for doubt or hesitation, rather it is positively certain that [the following day] is of Ramaḍān. He who formulates his intention during the night [and decides to fast the following day] and then eats while it is yet night will not invalidate his intention. If a woman in a state of menstruation should entertain the intention of fasting [on the following day] and her period come to an end before dawn, her fast would be valid.

The third duty is that, as long as he remembers that he is fasting, the individual should abstain (*imsāk*) from intentionally allowing any material substance, such as food, drink, snuff, and enema, to enter his body. All these render his fast invalid. It is not, however, invalidated by phlebotomy and cupping, nor by forcing the probe into the ear or the orifice of the penis unless the probe reaches the bladder. Whatever enters the body unintentionally, such as dust, flies, or water during the rinsing of the mouth will not invalidate the fast. Water which enters the body during the rinsing of the mouth, however, will invalidate the fast if the individual goes to excess in rinsing his mouth, because he would then be [deliberately] negligent. This is what we meant when we said intentionally. We said 'as long as he remembers that he is fasting' in order to exempt [from this ruling] the one who has forgotten that he was fasting and whose eating will not invalidate his fast. But if the person should intentionally eat either at the beginning or at the end of the day, and later find that his eating has encroached upon the actual period of daylight it would be his duty to make amends (*qaḍā'*). But if he should, to the best of his ability, continue to believe [that he had not eaten outside the prescribed time], he would not have to make amends. Yet he should not eat either in the early morning or in early evening except after careful and thorough examination [of the time].

The fourth duty is abstinence (*imsāk*) from sexual intercourse. The definition of sexual intercourse is the disappearance of the glans of the penis [in the vulva]. If the person, forgetting that he is fasting, should have sexual intercourse, he would not, because of it, break the fast. If, during the night, he should either have sexual intercourse or experience an erotic dream, and wake up in the morning in a state of impurity (*junub*), his fast would not thereof be broken. If the dawn breaks while he is copulating with his wife, and he stops immediately, his fast remains intact; but if he continues [until he reaches the orgasm] his fast will be invalidated, and atonement (*kaffārah*) becomes incumbent upon him.

The fifth duty is abstinence from deliberate seminal emission (*istimnā'*), either through sexual contact or through no sexual contact. For deliberate seminal emission breaks the fast. The person, however, will not break his fast if he kisses his wife or lies with her unless in so doing he emits the seminal fluid. Nevertheless both are disapproved except where the man be advanced in age and in full control of his impulses, in which case there will be no harm in kissing, although abstinence therefrom is better and more desirable. It he fears that as a result of kissing [and toying] he may emit the seminal fluid, and yet kisses with the result that the seminal fluid is emitted, he breaks his fast because he was [deliberately] negligent.

The sixth duty is abstinence from vomiting because it renders the fast invalid. But if one cannot help it, his fast remains intact and valid. And if a person swallows phlegm or mucus from his throat or chest he will not invalidate his fast. This has been made permissible because of the prevalence of the affliction. But if he swallows either after it had gotten to his mouth, he will break his fast.

The Duties Attending the Breaking of the Fast

The duties attending (*lawāzim*) the breaking of the fast are four, namely, making amends (*qaḍā'*), atonement (*kaffārah*), expiation (*fidyah*), and abstinence from food and drink for the rest of the day in imitation of those who are fasting.

Making amends (*qaḍā'*), is obligatory upon every responsible Muslim who has neglected to observe the fast with or without any excuse. Thus the menstruating woman, as well as the apostate, is under obligation to make amends for [every] fasting [which she or he fails to observe]; while the unbeliever, the minor, and the insane are under no such obligation. Making amends for days omitted in Ramaḍān need not be consecutively performed but may be performed either at different intervals or all at once.

The atonement (*kaffārah*), is not obligatory except after sexual intercourse. Seminal emission, food and drink require no atonement. The atonement consists of freeing one slave. If this is not possible, thefasting of two consecutive months will suffice; however, if this also be beyond the man's power he should feed sixty poor men, [giving] each a bushel [of wheat, or barley or dates].

As to abstinence from food and drink for the rest of the day, it is obligatory upon anyone who broke the fast [without any excuse] or failed to carry out [all its requirements]. This menstruating woman is under no obligation to fast for the rest of the day if she has already become pure. Similarly the traveller, who at the end of two days' journey, arrives not in a state of fasting, is under no obligation to fast for the rest of the day. It is also obligatory to obstain from food and drink on doubtful days when only one trustworthy witness has declared that he has seen the new moon. Furthermore, when on travel, unless it is unbearable, it is better to fast than not to fast No one should break his fast on the day when he embarks on a journey if he has already begun that day by fasting, nor on the day when he comes in from a journey, if he has already begun that day by fasting.

As to expiation (*fidyah*), it is obligatory upon pregnant and nursing women if they should not fast for the sake of their children. Besides making amends for days thus omitted, they should give in expiation a bushel of wheat to the poor for each day they did not fast. The aged man who does not fast [because of his infirmity] should give a bushel [of wheat] for every day thus omitted.

The Practices Connected with the Fast

The practices connected with the fast are six. They are delaying the time of the *suḥūr*,[1] speeding the breaking of the fast by eating dates or drinking water before performing prayer, putting away the toothpick after sunset, generous giving during the month of Ramaḍān especially because of its special excellences which were discussed in the Book on Almsgiving, special study of the Qur'ān, and retreating (*i'tikāf*) into the mosque especially during the last ten days of the month of Ramaḍān. It was the custom of the Apostle of God, upon the arrival of the last ten days of the month of Ramaḍān, to roll up his mattress, fasten his mantle around his waist [214], and, making his family do the same, continue in his worship [until the end of the ten-day period],[2] since during these ten days the Night of Power (*laylat al qadr*) falls. More probably the Night of Power falls on an odd night; most likely among these is the [twenty-] first, or the [twenty-] third, or the [twenty-] fifth, or the [twenty-] seventh. During

1. *Suḥūr* signifies the eating of the last meal which the fasting Muslim is allowed to have just before daybreak. The meal itself is called the *saḥūr*.

2. Al-Bukhārī, Laylat al-Qadr : 5.

this ten-day retreat, the continuous observance is preferred.

If the person vows or states his intention to observe these the days in retreat continuously, the continuity of his observance is broken if he leaves [the mosque] without [justifiable] necessity, such as leaving in order to call on some sick person, or to attend a funeral, or to visit a friend, or to renew his purification. But if he interrupts his retreat in order to answer a call of nature the continuity of his observance will not be broken. The person may, during the period of retreat, perform his ablutions at his [own] home, but he may not attend to any other work on his way [from and back to the mosque]. The Apostle of God was wont not to leave the mosque except for answering the call of nature, and on his way [from and back to the mosque], he did not inquire about the sick except as he passed by [without stopping].[1] The continuity of the observance of the retreat will be broken through sexual intercourse, but not through kissing. While in the mosque the person may use perfumes and contract marriage. [Continuity is not broken] through eating,

1. Abu-Dāwūd, I'tikāf : 4.

sleeping, and washing of the hands in a basin because they are all [unavoidable and] necessary. Nor is it broken by the emergence of a part of the body [from the mosque], for the Apostle of God was wont to put his head out to be massaged by 'Ā'ishah' who was in an [adjacent] chamber.[1] Whenever the person leaves his retreat in order to answer a call of nature, he should restate his intention upon returning to resume the retreat, unless he had stated his intention for the ten day period in advance. Despite this, however, the renewal of the intention is better.

1. Al-Bukhārī, I'tikāf : 19.

SECTION II

On the Mysteries of Fasting and its Inward Conditions

Now that fasting is of three [successive] grades, namely, the fasting of the general public (*ṣawm al-'umūm*), the fasting of the select few (*ṣawm al-khuṣūs*), and the fasting of the elite among the select few (*ṣawm khuṣūṣ al-khuṣuṣ*).

The fasting of the general public involves refraining from satisfying the appetite of the stomach and the appetite of the sex, as has already been discussed.

The fasting of the select few is to keep the ears, the eyes, the tongue, and hands, and the feet as well as the other senses free from sin.

The fasting of the elite among the select few is the fast of the heart from mean thoughts and worldly worries and its complete unconcern with anything but God. Such a fast is broken by thinking on anything other than God and the last day, as well as by concern over this world, except in so far as it promotes religion which belongs to the hereafter. Thus those whose hearts are sanctified have said, "He who spends his day worrying over what he will have for breaking his fast sins." This is because he has little confidence in the bounty of God and little faith that the livelihood promised unto him will be received. In this rank stand the prophets, the saints and the favourites of God the most high. We shall not dwell very long on the verbal description of the kind of fasting but shall define it through its active operation. It is to seek God with all of one's strength and to turn away from all other things besides Him. In short it is to embody the words of God when He said, "Say 'God', then leave them in their pastime of cavillings."[1]

The fasting of the select few, which is the fasting of the virtuous men, is to keep the senses free from sin and is accomplished through six things: To refrain from looking at anything blameworthy and disapproved, or anything which occupies the person and diverts him from remembering God. The Apostle said, "The coveting glance is one of the poisoned arrows of the devil. He who for fear of God abstains therefrom will

1. *Sūrah* vi : 91.

receive from Him a belief the sweetness of which will fill his heart."[1]

Jābir[2] related on the authority of Anas that the Apostle of God once said, "Five things break the fast : the telling of lies, backbiting, tale-bearing, perjury, and the casting of coveting and lustful eyes."[3]

The second is to keep the tongue free from raving, lying, backbiting, tale-bearing, obscenity, abusive speech, wrangling, and hypocrisy, and to impose silence upon it. Furthermore it should be employed in the remembrance and glorification of God and engaged in reading of the Qur'ān. Of such is the fasting of the tongue. We have it on the authority of Bishr ibn-al-Ḥārith that Sufyān [al-Thawri] once said, "Backbiting renders fasting of no effect." Quoting Mujāhid, Layth[4] once said, "Two traits render fasting of no effect: backbiting and lying."

The Apostle of God said, "Verily, fasting is like unto a shield; therefore whenever one of

1. Unidentified.

2. Perhaps Jābir ibn-'Abdullāh al-Anṣāri.

3. Unidentified.

4. Ibn abi-Sulaym, died between A.H. 136 and 143/A.D. 754 and 760. *Cf.* ibn-Sa'd, Vol VI, pp. 243-44 ; ibn-Qutaybah, p. 241 ; *Shadharāt al-Dhahab*, Vol. I, pp. 207, 212.

you fasteth let him not speak unseemly or act foolishly. If anyone disputeth with him or sweareth at him, let him say, 'I am fasting, verily I am fasting'."[1] In another tradition we read about two women who lived during the lifetime of the Apostle. As they were fasting one day the pangs of hunger and the darts of thirst proved too much for them to endure, and they almost collapsed. Consequently they sent to the Apostle of God asking him permission to break their fast. In reply he sent them a cup saying, "Vomit into this cup what ye have eaten." [215] To the amazement of all present the one filled half the cup with pure blood and tender flesh and the other filled up the second half of the cup with the same thing. Thereupon the Apostle said, "These two women have fasted from that which God hath made lawful unto them and have broken their fast by doing that which He hath made unlawful unto them. They sat down and engaged in backbiting. The flesh and blood which they vomited is the flesh and blood of those people whom they have traduced."[2]

1. Al-Bukhāri, Ṣawm : 2.
2. Unidentified.

The third is to close the ears to every reprehensible thing because everything which is unlawful to utter is also unlawful to hear. For this reason God regarded the listener and the 'sharks' of unlawful trade alike when He said, "Listeners to falsehood, 'sharks' of the unlawful trade."[1] And again, "Had not the masters and the 'divines' forbidden their uttering wickedness and devouring unlawful trade, bad indeed would have been their deeds."[2] Silence therefore, in the face of backbiting is unlawful. Said God, "Ye are, then, like unto them."[3] The Apostle also said, "The backbiter and he who listens unto him are partners in sin."[4]

The fourth is constraining the rest of the senses from sins, restraining the hand from reaching evil, and curbing the foot from pursuing wickedness, as well as avoiding questionable foods at the break of the fast. Otherwise, if the fast is going to be abstinence from lawful things and partaking, on breaking the fast, of unlawful things, it will have no significance at all. Such a fasting

1. *Sūrah* v : 46.
2. *Sūrah* v : 68.
3. *Sūrah* iv : 139.
4. Unidentified.

man is like one who builds a cabin but destroys a capital.[1] For lawful food is harmful not because of its quality but because of its quantity and fasting is designed to induce moderation. Similarly the person who, for fear of the bad effect of an excessive does of medicine, resorts to taking a dose of poison, is indeed foolish. The unlawful is poison detrimental to religion while the lawful is like a medicine a little of which is beneficial but the excess of which is harmful. The purpose of fasting is to induce moderation therein. The Apostle of God said, "Many a man gets nothing out of his fast except hunger and thirst."[2] In explanation of this it has been said that [the Apostle] meant the person who breaks his fast on unlawful things. Others said that he meant the person who abstains from lawful food and breaks his fast on the flesh of men through backbiting which is unlawful. Still others said that the Apostle meant the person who does not keep his senses free from sin.

The fifth is that when breaking his fast, a person should not overeat of [even] the lawful food, thereby stuffing his belly full. For there is no

1. Lit. builds a castle and destroys a region.

2. Ibn-Mājah, Ṣiyām : 21.

vessel more abominable unto God than a belly stuffed with lawful food. How could any one expect to overcome the enemy of God and subdue his own appetite through fasting if, when he breaks his fast, he compensates himself for what he had missed during the day and even helps himself to more foods and drinks of diverse kinds. It has thus become the custom to store up all the food for the month of Ramaḍān, wherein more food and drink are devoured than in several months. Yet it is well known that the purpose of fasting is hunger and the suppression of lust so that the soul might be able to attain piety. If the stomach were not given any food from the early morning until the evening so that its appetite became aroused and its desire increased and then it were fed with delicacies and stuffed to satiety therewith, its pleasure would be enhanced and vitality doubled, consequently giving rise to passions otherwise dormant. The spirit as well as the secret of fasting is to weaken the flesh which is Satan's tool for turning men back to evil. [Such weakening of the flesh] is never achieved unless a person reduces his food to the amount of food which he would have eaten in the evening if he were not fasting. But if, on breaking his fast, he should eat an amount of food equivalent to what he would have eaten during both the daytime and the evening, he would reap no benefit from his fast. As a matter of fact among the proprieties of fasting is that the person should not sleep much during the daytime but rather stay up so that he might feel the pangs of hunger and the flames of thirst and become conscious of the weakness of the flesh, with the result that his heart would be cleansed and purified. He should maintain his flesh in such a state of weakness during the Night of Power so that he might find his night worship (*tahajjud*) easier to perform and his [night] portions (sing. *wird*) easier to read. It is hoped, then, that Satan will not hover around his heart and that he will be able to lift his eyes unto the kingdom of heaven. In this connexion the Night of Power represents the night on which a glimpse of the invisible world is revealed to man. It is also the night which is alluded to by the words of God when He said, "Verily We have sent it down on the Night of Power."[1]

He who buries his head deep into a nose-bag full of food cannot hope to see the invisible world.

1. *Sūrah* xcvii : 1.

Even if he keeps his stomach empty he will not be able to remove the veil and see the invisible world unless he also empties his mind from everything except God. This is the whole matter, the basis of which is to cut down the amount of food one eats. This will be further discussed in the book on the various kinds of food.

The sixth is that, after breaking the fast, his heart should remain in a state of suspense between fear and hope since he does not know whether his fast will be accepted, and consequently he will be one of the favourites of God, or rejected, and he will be one of those who have incurred divine disfavour. He should remain in such a state of suspense after every act of worship.

It has been related that al-Ḥasan ibn-abi al-Ḥasan [Yasār] al-Baṣri once passed by a group of men who were rollicking and laughing and said unto them, "Verily God has made the month of Ramaḍān a race-course where men compete in His worship. Some have won their race and were crowned with success, while others lagged behind and lost. We are surprised and astonished at the man who wastes his time in indolence and laughter on the day when the earnest finish victorious and the idle meet with failure and disaster. By God, if the veil were to be removed you will find the good man occupied with his good works and the evil-doer with his evil deeds." In other words the joy of the man whose fast has been accepted will occupy him and keep him from indolence, while the agony and regrets of the man whose fast has been rejected will take all joy from his heart and make laughter impossible.

It was related on the authority of al-Aḥnaf ibn-Qays that he was once told, [216] "Thou art an old and aged man, and fasting would make thee weak." To which he replied, "This fast is my preparation for a long journey. Verily to endure the yoke of God's service is easier than to endure the yoke of His torture." Such words depict the inward meaning of fasting.

If you then ask, "How can the jurisprudents approve the fasting of a person who confines himself to restraining the appetite of his stomach and the urge of his sex instinct, but neglects these inward aspects of the fast; how, then, can they say that his fast is valid?" Then know that the jurisprudents of the outward law support its formal requirements by means of proofs far weaker than those with which we established its inward conditions, especially those of backbiting and the like. At any rate the jurisprudents of the outward Law are not expected to concern themselves with any obligations other than those which are within the reach of the ordinary common folk who are occupied with the affairs of this world. On the other hand the learned men of the hereafter mean by validity acceptance and by acceptance the achievement of the intended purpose. By the purpose intended in fasting they understood the taking over of one of the qualities of God, namely, endurance (*ṣamadīyah*) as well as following in the example of the angels by refraining, as much as possible, from carnal lust. For the angels are not subject to carnal lust while man, by virtue of his ability to overcome lust through the light of reason, stands above the animals [which possess no such light]. On the other hand, because he is subject to carnal lust and is judged by his ability to fight [its temptations], he stands below the angels [who are free from them]. The more he indulges in lust the lower he descends and the closer he comes to the level of the animals. The more he suppresses his lust the higher he ascends and the closer he comes to the level of the angels. The angels stand in close proximity to God, and whoever follows in their footsteps and emulates their example draws like them nigh unto God. But this proximity (*qurb*) is not one of location but one of qualities and attributes.

If, among the men of insight and the physicians of the heart, this be the secret of fasting, what good-will there be in delaying a meal and combining two at sunset while indulging in the satisfaction of all the other physical desires and lusts throughout the day? And if there were good in such a behaviour what would the words of the Apostle when he said, "Many a man gets nothing out of his fast except hunger and thirst,"[1] mean? For this reason abu-al-Dardā' once said, "How good is the sleep of the wise men and how excellent is their eating; behold how they put to shame the wakefulness of the foolish and their fasting. Verily the weight of an atom of the worship of the faithful and pious is better than the weight of mountains of the worship of those who are misguided [and those in error]." Consequently one of the learned men said, "Many a fasting man is not truly fasting, and many a man not

1. Ibn-Mājah, Ṣiyām : 21.

abstaining from food and drink is truly fasting." The man who is truly fasting while not abstaining from food and drink is he who keeps himself free from sin; and the fasting man who is not truly fasting is he who, while he hungers and thirsts, allows himself every freedom in sin. But every one who truly understands fasting and its secret knows that he who abstains from food, drink, and sexual intercourse but commits [all manner of] sins is like the person who, in performing the ablution runs his hand over one of his members thrice, thereby outwardly fulfilling the Law as far as the member is concerned, but neglecting the truly important thing which is the actual washing. Consequently because of his ignorance, his prayer is rejected. On the other hand, he who breaks the fast through eating but observes it by keeping himself free from sin is like the person who, in performing the ablution, washes each of the members of his body once only. His prayers are, by the will of God, accepted because he has fulfilled the principal thing in the ablution although he has failed to fulfil the details. But he who does both is like the person who, in performing the ablution, washes each member of his body thrice, thereby fulfilling both the principal purpose of ablution as well as its elaborate details, which constitutes perfection. The Apostle once said, "Verily fasting is a trust; let each, therefore, take good care of his trust."[1] Again when he recited, "Verily God enjoineth you to give back your trusts to their owners,"[2] he raised his hands and touching his ears and eyes said, "[The gift of] hearing and [the gift of] seeing are each a trust [from God]." Similarly [the gift of speech is a trust], for if it were not so the Apostle would not have said, "If anyone disputeth with another and sweareth at him let the latter say, 'I am fasting, verily I am fasting'."[3] Or in other words, "I have been interested with this my tongue in order to keep and hold, not in order to give it free rein in retort and reply to thee."

It is clear, then, that every act of worship is possessed of an outward form and an inner [secret], an external husk and internal pith. The husks are of different grades and each grade has different layers. It is for you to choose whether to be content with the husk or join the company of the wise and the learned.

1. Unidentified.
2. *Sūrah* iv: 61.
3. *Cf.* al Bukhāri, Ṣawm, 2.

SECTION III

On Voluntary Fasting and the Arrangement of Portions therein

Know that the desirability of fasting becomes more certain on special days of particular excellence. These days of excellence recur either annually, or monthly, or weekly.

Besides those of Ramaḍān, the annual days of excellence are the day of ʻArafah (*Yawm ʻArafah*),[1] the day of ʻĀshūrā' (*Yawm ʻĀshūrā'*),[2] the first ten[3] days of Dhu-al-Ḥijjah, and the first ten days of al-Muḥarram. Similarly the sacred months[4] are, in their entirety, a fitting time for fasting, and of special excellence.

The Apostle of God was in the habit of frequently fasting during [the month of] Shaʻbān to the extent where it would be thought that he was

1. The ninth day of Dhu-al-Ḥijjah when the pilgrim proceeds to Mount ʻArafāt in order to observe the vigil of the feast of sacrifice (*Īd al-Aḍḥa*).

2. The tenth day of al-Muḥarram.

3. Actually only the first nine days ending with the day of ʻArafah are included.

4. Dhu-al-Qaʻdah, Dhu-al-Ḥijjah, al-Muḥarram, and Rajab.

in Ramaḍān.[1] In another tradition [we read], "Besides the month of Ramaḍān the most excellent month for fasting is the month of God [217] al-Muḥarram."[2] This is because al-Muḥarram is the first month of the year; hence, to commence the year right is more pleasing to God and gives greater hope that His blessing will continue through. The Apostle also said, "The fast of one single day during a sacred month is more excellent than the fast of thirty days during another; and the fast of one single day during Ramaḍān is more excellent than that of thirty days during another sacred month."[3] In another tradition we have, "He who fasts three days —Thursday, Friday, and Saturday—during a sacred month, will be credited by God with nine hundred years of worship for each day."[4] And again, "When the 'ides' of Sha'bān are gone, there should be no fasting until Ramaḍān is on."[5] It is therefore desirable that one should, if he were fasting during Sha'bān, break his fast a few days before the beginning of Ramaḍān. But if

1. Cf. al-Bukhārī, Ṣawm : 52.
2. Al-Nasā'i, Qiyām al-Layl : 6.
3. Unidentified.
4. Unidentified.
5. Al-Tirmidhi, Ṣawm : 38.

he should continue his fast through Sha'bān into Ramaḍān his action will be perfectly permissible since the Apostle of God himself has done that once, although, ordinarily, he allowed a period of no fasting to intervene.[1] Nor is it permissible for him to prepare for the arrival of Ramaḍān with a fast of two or three days from Sha'bān unless he observes the corresponding portions.

Some of the Companions disapproved of fasting the whole of the month of Rajab lest it would become equal to the month of Ramaḍān in excellence and importance. The excellent months (*al-ashhur al-fāḍilah*) are Dhu-al-Ḥijjah, al-Muḥarram, Rajab, and Sha'bān while the sacred months (*al-ashhur al-ḥurum*) are Dhu-al-Qa'dah, Dhu-al-Ḥijjah, al-Muḥarram, and Rajab. Of these one, [i.e., Rajab], stands alone, and three follow successively one after the other. The most excellent of these is Dhu-al-Ḥijjah because in it fall the appointed days (*al-ayyām al-ma'lūmāt*) and the numbered days (*al-ayyām al-ma'dūdāt*). Dhu-al-Qa'dah is one of the sacred months as well as one of the months of pilgrimage. On the other hand Shawwāl is one of the months of

1. Abu-Dāwūd, Ṣawm : 11.

pilgrimage but not one of the sacred months, while neither al-Muḥarram nor Rajab is a month of pilgrimage.

The Apostle, as we see it recorded in the following tradition, once said, "No good works are more excellent or more acceptable to God than those which are performed during the [first] ten days of Dhu-al-Ḥijjah. Verily the fast on one of these days is equal to the fast of one whole year, and the prayer during one of these nights is equivalent to the prayer during the Night of Power (*laylat al-qadr*)." He was then asked, "Not even holy war for the cause of God is better?" To which he replied, "Not even holy war for the cause of God is better except when the person's steed is killed and his own blood is shed."[1]

The excellent days which recur every month are the first, the middle, and the last days of each month. In the middle of each month fall the days of the bright nights (*al-ayyām al bīḍ*). These are the thirteenth, the fourteenth, and the fifteenth days of each month.[2]

1. Al-Tirmidhi, Ṣawm : 52.
2. *Cf.* al-Bukhāri, Ṣawm . 60 ; al-Tirmidhi, Ṣawm : 54.

The excellent days which recur every week are Monday, Thursday, and Friday. These are the excellent days of the week on which it is desirable to fast and do good since, because of the special beneficence of these days, the reward of the acts performed thereon is multiplied double-fold.

As to life-long fasting (*ṣawm al-dahr*) it is all-inclusive. Mystics (*ṣālikūn*) hold different views concerning it. Some of them, basing their opinion on several traditions,[1] have viewed it with disfavour. The truth of the matter is that it is viewed with disfavour for two reasons : the one is that, by fasting the whole duration of his life, the person will have to abstain from eating even on the two feasts,[2] [namely the feast of Ramaḍān (*al-Fiṭr*) and the feast of Sacrifice (*al-Aḍḥa*) as well as on the days of orientation (*ayyām al-tashrīq*) ;[3] the other is that by so doing, he departs from the established practice of the Apostle and makes fasting a yoke for himself although God would like him to enjoy his liberties just as much as He would want him to fulfil his obliga-

1. *Cf.* al-Tirmidhi, Ṣawm : 56 ; al-Bukhāri, Ṣawm : 56.
2. See al-Tirmidhi, Ṣawm : 58.
3. *Ibid.*, Ṣawm : 59.

tions. If, however, there are no such [dangers] and the person deems it good for himself to observe a life-long fast, let him by all means do so since several of the Companions and the followers have done the same. The Apostle, according to a tradition related by Abu-Musa al-Ash'ari,[1] said, "He who observes a life-long fast has no place in Hell, and will live to the ripe age of ninety."[2]

There is, however, besides the life-long fast, and beneath it in merit, another state, namely, fasting on alternate days (*ṣawm niṣf al-dahr*). It is harder to observe and more effective in mortifying the flesh. Several traditions in praise of its excellence have been related, especially relative to the state of the fasting servant who fasts one day and enjoys the blessings of God on the other. The Apostle said, "The keys to the coffers of the world and the treasures of the earth have been offered to me but I declined to accept them saying, 'I had better hunger one day and be full another. When I am full my praise shall I offer

1. One of the two umpires at the alleged arbitration after Siffīn. He died A.H.52/A.D. 672, Ibn-Qutaybah, pp. 135-36 ; ibn-Sa'd, Vol. IV, pp. 78-86, Vol. VI, p. 9.

2. Al-Ṭayālisi : 513, 514.

unto God and when I hunger unto Him shall I offer my supplications'."[1] And again, "The most excellent fasting is that of my brother David ; he was wont to fast one day and omit the other."[2]

Of the same nature is the Apostle's argument with 'Abdullāh ibn-'Amr[3] on the subject of fasting. 'Abdullāh, replying to one of the suggestions of the Apostle, said, "I can stand a more [strenuous] fast than that." Thereupon the Apostle retorted, "Fast on alternate days." But again 'Abdullāh said, "I want something more excellent." To which the Apostle replied, "There is nothing which is more excellent than that."[4] It has also been related that the Apostle of God never fasted a whole month except in Ramaḍān."[5]

He who is unable to fast on alternate days (*niṣf al-dahr*) throughout his entire life may try to fast every third day (*thulth al-dahr*) ; i.e., he may fast on one day and break the fast on the following

1. *Cf.* al-Tirmidhi, Zuhd : 35.
2. *Cf.* al-Bukhāri, Ṣawm : 56, 58, 59.
3. Ibn-al-'Āṣ, A H. 65/A.D. 684-85 : ibn-Sa'd, Vol. IV, pt. 2, pp. 8-13, Vol. VII, pt. 2, pp 189-90.
4. Al-Bukhāri, Ṣawm : 56, 58, 59; *cf.* ibn-Sa'd Vol. IV, pt 2, p. 9.
5. Al-Bukhāri, Ṣawm : 53.

two, and so on. Again if a person fasts for three days at the beginning of the month, three at the middle, and three at the end of the month, he will have fasted one-third of his entire life and his fasting days will coincïde with the excellent seasons. If he fasts on Monday, Thursday and Friday [of every week] he will approximate the one-third.

If the excellent seasons have been determined, the real meaning of fasting will have to be understood before attaining perfection. The main purpose of fasting is to purify the heart and to concentrate all its attention upon God. Those versed in the science of the subtleties of the inner [self] examine its different conditions; for possibly it may require continued fasting, or uninterrupted fasting, or a mixture of both.

If, however, the individual comprehends the real meaning of fasting and, through the observation of his own heart, ascertains its place and value in the journey on the road to the hereafter, he will not fail to find out where the welfare of his heart lies. This does not necessitate a continuous routine. For this reason it has been related that the Apostle was wont to fast until everyone thought that he never ate, and he used to eat until everyone thought that he never fasted. Similarly he was wont to sleep until everybody thought that he never woke up and used to stay up until everybody thought that he never went to bed.[1] In all this he was guided by the light of prophecy which revealed to him the proper conduct for every occasion and season.

Some of the learned men have viewed with disfavour the practice of allowing more than four days to intervene between each fast. This is just about equal to the period of feasting after Ramaḍān [or the feast of Sacrifice] and to the days of orientation (*ayyām al-tashrīq*). They pointed out that such a practice would harden the heart, give rise to bad habits, and increase the possibilities of passion and lust. In my opinion this is true of most people, especially those who eat twice every day and night.

This is what we have planned to discuss concerning the routine of voluntary fasting.

1. *Cf.* al-Bukhāri, Ṣawm : 53.

BIBLIOGRAPHY

Athīr, ibn-al-, *al-Kāmil fi-'l-Tārīkh* (Cairo, 1303).
Balādhuri, al-, *Ansāb al-Ashrāf*, ed. M. Ḥamīd Allāh (Cairo, 1959).
Bukhāri, al-, *Saḥīḥ* (Būlāq, 1296).
Dāwūd, abu-, *Sunan* (Cairo, 1280).
Hishām, ibn-, *Sīrat Rasūl Allāh*, ed. F. Wüstenfeld (Leyden, 1858-1860).
'Imād al-Ḥanbali, ibn-al-, *Shadharāt al-Dhahab fi Akhbār man Dhahab* (Cairo, 1350).
Mājah, ibn-, *Sunan* (Cairo, 1349).
Muslim, *Ṣaḥīḥ*, Delhi 1319; Dār al-Ṭibā'ah al-'Āmmah (Cairo, 1330).
Nasā'i, al-, *al-Mujtaba* (Delhi, 1315).
Qutaybah, ibn-, *Kitāb al-Ma'ārif*, ed. F. Wüstenfeld (Göttingen, 1850).
Sa'd, ibn-, *Kitāb al-Ṭabaqāt al-Kubra*, ed. E. Sachau and others (Leyden, 1905-21).
Tayālisi, al-, *Musnad* (Hyderabad, 1321).
Tirmidhi, al-, *Sunan* (Cairo, 1290).

INDEX OF PROPER NAMES AND SPECIAL TERMS